REACHING REACTIONS

A COLLECTION OF POETIC AFFIRMATIONS
365 DAYS OF PROFOUND AWAKENINGS

DANIELLE TIANO

REACHING REACTIONS:

A Collection of Poetic Affirmations
365 Days of Profound Awakenings

Copyright 2020 Danielle Tiano

Published by

WINGS
PUBLISHING

ISBN: 978-0-578-78409-0

Printed in the United States.

TO MY CHERISHED COMMUNITY

I kindly invite you to an unfolding journey into exploring where a single word, and the meaning it encompasses, can take you. My wish is that this collection prepares you to see through open eyes while awakening the understanding and knowledge in yourself and others, thereby enriching your life and allowing you to grow from these experiences. Powerful lessons are tucked inside each page. It is my honor to inspire you—to highlight the transforming forces that embrace our lives each day.

Poetry is an enriching and transforming shared platform where someone, everyone, is able to find a piece of themselves reflected in what they read. Once in a while, if we are lucky enough, we find a piece of literature so exquisitely revealing, we can't help but lose ourselves in it. Emanating from the pages are whimsical, lyrical words that genuinely elevate different interpretations.

The compositions that follow share a revival and advancement, requiring us to look within and articulate the emotionality of the seasons of life we encounter. *Reaching Reactions* is meant to help readers find meaning in their everyday moments. It should be read slowly, perhaps one affirmation each day, to allow you to sit with it, absorb its depth, interpret its meaning, and allow its illumination to penetrate from the first pronouncement to the final induction. Be contemplative and celebrate the fluidity in its beckoning.

~ DANIELLE TIANO

TABLE OF CONTENTS

CHAPTER ONE
LOVE

{LOVE}

It floats in and out of our existence like the clouds above us, moving in the direction it wishes. It changes, grows and evolves, deepening and dissolving at the very same time.

{LOVE}

We are surrounded, touched and influenced by it. Without fair warning, it drags us into its web until we drop all resistance and fall into its intended match, ready and willing to start our happily ever after.

{LOVE}

It is always searching for those who understand it, who welcome it. Mankind puts great faith in it, waiting for the moment in time when it chooses them.

{LOVE}

We have been woven into its world as it has been woven into ours. We cannot survive without it or it without us. Those who struggle to open themselves up to it or reject its comings will be haunted by its mystery and yearn to understand it.

{LOVE}

We all inhabit its world, though it does not always live in ours. It can heal our wounds, and expand our heart, knowing that its power will bring us together and not pull us apart.

{LOVE}

Its power is in the hope it delivers to each of us when it arrives, without a glimpse of where it came from in its current form.

{LOVE}

It consistently reminds us that when it arrives, it is something new and unlike anything we have ever experienced before. It is constantly changing and molding itself into its new life. The one component that remains, is its ability to ignite our fire and blow out that same flame at any given moment.

{LOVE}

It rejoices in romance, passion and desire, and those who lean in and embrace its complexity, will live a life filled with affection.

{LOVE}

It has an essence of its own; each of its intended connections holds a special purpose and kindred exchange.

{LOVE}

It comes and goes as it pleases. It influences us; we are dominated by its power, and without warning, it can change us, and challenge our trust in ourselves and others.

{LOVE}

It puts itself first, and the affection that pours into our hearts stems from its vibrational pull that spreads throughout the infinite universe.

{LOVE}

It is forceful with high expectations. It has always carried the deepest of emotions, though not as a human, but as love.

{LOVE}

Its strength is in its passion of impacting connections between two people, molding their hearts together, turning a "me" into a "we."

{LOVE}

It is forever changing, blossoming, living, dying and re-creating itself.

CHAPTER TWO

THE MIND

{THE MIND}

We ask it for permission to engage, make mistakes, stumble and fall through its complexity, heading toward expansion through insight and attitude. It takes concentrated thought into its force field, and when unleashed, it turns everything into celebration or altercation.

{THE MIND}

It causes an endless range of human censorship that does not fit accurately into our experiences.

{THE MIND}

It speaks to us readily to cancel or accept our thoughts at any given moment. It usually comes in the form of a critic, or old negative programing, balancing our beliefs between what is false and what is true. It houses our scrambled emotions between confusion and certainty.

{THE MIND}

Every time a thought is shared, it reveals the image we project to the world. It is always renewing through current information and speculations that scramble our mental stories with no cataloged understanding in sight.

{THE MIND}

It can be rooted with problem-solving capacity and resolve situations at a rapid rate. It is complex like a tapestry woven with beauty and historical markings, artfully proclaiming life in each thread.

{THE MIND}

It evaluates the importance of the physical form of ourselves and others. It pushes against patience, debating the nexus where questions meet answers.

{THE MIND}

It's forever controlling, and infinitely powerful. It believes its thoughts to be true, and we readily place our certainty in it. It contributes to our reasoning and advancement. It analyzes itself through the thoughts with which we are at war.

{THE MIND}

It's forever changing, evolving and expanding, although thoughts may creep in to stall its progress. It brews questions, seeks answers, and ponders lessons learned.

{THE MIND}

It challenges our inner critic by focusing on our flaws and failures. It's competitive by nature, always seeking knowledge and capable of distorted perspective, sometimes clear and sometimes blurry.

{THE MIND}

It often confuses feelings with reasoning. It occupies the core of our existence and needs constant input to continue to grow. Keep it challenged, keep it learning, and keep it healthy and safe in its appreciative, traveling home.

{THE MIND}

It can be an instrument of joy or sorrow, of wakening or slumber. It is evident that our thoughts reveal our truths, and over time, our communication exposes that which we believe to be true.

{THE MIND}

When directed on pushing positively toward joy and happiness, it can soar in celebration. Although in moments of doubt, we need to redirect it, reassuring ourselves that our hopes are contained within it.

{THE MIND}

It calculates thoughts into reasoning, and understanding into love, compassionate in its reflection, yet deceptive and damaging when concerned only with protecting its own identity.

CHAPTER THREE
ATTITUDE

{ATTITUDE}

It is always looking to take ownership, for a way to control how we express ourselves and communicate that which is all-consuming and incomparable to other parts of our makeup.

{ATTITUDE}

Its subtlety speaks volumes to its audience, a true master at making a point. It becomes our permanent mark on the world, inscribed dialogue in our minds, forever flaunting, never invisible.

{ATTITUDE}

It can be adopted in a negative or positive framework; it's the action that follows it that determines our experience and, if not previously chosen, it will decide its most submissive direction.

{ATTITUDE}

It's never silent; it's loud like thunder, projecting our character to those who hear it, and ultimately revealing the way we are perceived.

{ATTITUDE}

It exposes our true self, the one usually hidden behind our own mental critic; it is a shared story, incomplete until someone whispers back with their interpretation.

{ATTITUDE}

It commands our mouth to speak, our voice to amplify, and our mind to question it, and when it's suppressed, it is kept silent and starving.

{ATTITUDE}

When we give power to it, it can trigger a spark that travels like a small missile in one direction with no regard to the destruction it may leave behind.

{ATTITUDE}

It's something learned and something inherited, always changing and constantly challenged.

{ATTITUDE}

It can express negative or positive beliefs, question motives and confuse others by that which we express.

{ATTITUDE}

We may not recognize our own temperament, but it marks us endlessly wherever we go.

{ATTITUDE}

It dictates how others perceive us and
seeks the individual who chooses it.

{ATTITUDE}

Care for it, listen to it, seek to understand it, but above all else, nurture it so that it makes the most positive statement.

{ATTITUDE}

It cannot remain hidden, as it is forever rising to the surface.

{ATTITUDE}

It can be the deciding difference to every outcome in which we participate. When positive, it can prompt calmness, a peace that clings to us forever; when negative, it can infect us like a cruel plague.

{ATTITUDE}

It can be toxic or triumphant, but it will
ultimately be the entirety of who we are.

{ATTITUDE}

It's the core of our being, the starting point of all our behaviors. Good or bad, it drives our identity and the way we conduct our lives.

{ATTITUDE}

It is shared in the beginning of every exchange and again in the end. It is one of the most important measures of our being, as it is our message to the world…

{ATTITUDE}

It can revise the way our mind reviews what has happened and challenge our mental tendency to get angry or offended. It indulges our emotions and conveys what other people hear.

CHAPTER FOUR

WHEN

{WHEN}

We think that if we reach an understanding from the message it whispers, we will no longer question our motives, unaware that it is a false sense of assurance, like a flickering candle that never fully illuminates.

{WHEN}

It's the mistrust we must release, giving up all ties to its questioning power that follows our every inquiry. It ceases our progress by the doubt it pours into our anticipation. We automatically reach for it, wanting it to guide us out of our uncertainty, but it hinders our outcomes and stalls our ability to move forward.

{WHEN}

It magnifies our anxiety and rattles us to the core until we increase our questioning capacity. We need to look beyond it and start asking ourselves the right questions fueled by hope, like existential riddles wrapped in faith, giving them a wider perspective, lessening its stability.

{WHEN}

We struggle with it, fight it, questioning every punch we receive in its contentious ring. It surely has the power to dim our light by the restrictions it places on our choices. It always comes after we are needing the reason, though its ancient roots are so deeply ingrained into our interpretation, that we must surrender or be forever stained by its effects.

{WHEN}

It follows us like our shadow, always there, invading our thought process, nagging us to take notice and surrender to its false power. Like a loud outburst, screaming its importance and pushing us toward the course it wishes. We think it will harmonize us, that it will calm our worries and take us to a place where time is not a burden.

{WHEN}

It constructs the rising walls that barricade us from moving forward, increasing our momentum to face the worry that follows it.

{WHEN}

It has stolen the many years we have wasted on it, functioning best where we feel weak, and centered in doubt. It forces us to surrender to its misplaced power with the unanswered questions we keep tucked deep inside.

{WHEN}

It's the perceived delay toward the interpretation we seek. It questions our power, and then an opportunity arises, teaching us to be patient, to learn, and to listen to the silence that offers its concealed interpretation.

{WHEN}

It tangles our thoughts, binding us to its magnitude, hindering our progress with no explanation in sight. It padlocks us to its unpredictability and attaches hidden agendas that we will never have the ability to reach.

{WHEN}

It comes full force when everything we thought to be true crumbles into so many pieces that the recovery is not achievable. We overplay it, and then we are always surprised when the timing is not in alignment with our expectations.

{WHEN}

We experience a constant sense of shock and disappointment by its sting and the permanent mark it leaves on our lives if not answered.

{WHEN}

It's the most asked question we pray for; it is our struggle to trust in the Lord when we feel like He is not punctual or keeping His promises. We must give up our control, trust and lean into God, and stop wasting our time asking a question that has no defined explanation.

{WHEN}

The word tortures us like a falsely accused prisoner trying to prove his innocence. It pulls at us like a knotted rope, so tightly woven that there is no chance of it ever unraveling the competing thoughts that enter our mind.

CHAPTER FIVE

CHOICES

{CHOICES}

They are unpredictable, like an unexpected casualty that comes in, shakes us up, and complicates the thoughts we ponder. They question our motives like a commanding force, doubting us, pressing a heavy weight upon our soul.

{CHOICES}

If we sit in stillness, we will discover that the sound that lives there is trying to clear the path toward that which was designed for us.

{CHOICES}

They leave us as fast as they come, like bricks being laid one by one, permanent in their existence, yet suspended in the moment, like roots with nowhere to grow.

{CHOICES}

When married with doubt, they ignite like fire, which burns rapidly over everything in its path—painted in colorful mental formations, animated and active in our decision-making.

{CHOICES}

They enter with a whispering tone, yet demand our attention, questioning our reasoning, stealing the silence from our minds.

{CHOICES}

They reveal the altercations before we speak; our thoughts are tangled between the words affectionately caressing our tongue with joy, and the contentions that are sharp, stinging us from the fears of our past.

{CHOICES}

We wish to be a stranger to our sorrows, letting them go, like the waves that lose themselves in the ocean's current. The beauty that prevails in them is that they can be adjusted, altered or reinvented.

{CHOICES}

Into the vague depths we ponder, working through the process of our entanglement between right and wrong, grasping for one that feels true. We reach deep into our gut for answers, answers that have been guarded by our concealed motives.

{CHOICES}

We must give birth to their revival or let them go, falling to their death. Failure to make a choice is also a choice. In the end, we must surrender to them, confident that we have done the best we can, awaiting the final outcome, and hoping we will celebrate each one of them.

{CHOICES}

The moment reflection is demanded, our truths will be revived toward our expressed understandings. As the lessons are learned, they will lay hold of our mind, eager and ready to release.

{CHOICES}

There is a voice that lives inside us, screaming, "Listen to me, to my joy, to my sorrow; listen to my reasoning," and if we question that call that lives in our gut, we often make the wrong one.

{CHOICES}

We cannot take them back, change them, or fix them; they become a continuation of our being, like shadows trailing us wherever we go…

{CHOICES}

They are happening all around us, within us, and are endlessly being modified outside of our control.

{CHOICES}

They can lead us to happiness and joy, or sorrow and shame—it's all in the outcome of the decisions we make. The mind meets them at each crossing, lucid and lastingly tinted by the attachments that hold onto them.

{CHOICES}

The ones we make can either cage us or set us free, believing and knowing everything is meant to be. We can live in the joy and celebration of our decisions, sitting confidently in them, or we can be cemented in the pain from what they have constructed. But either way, we will gain new knowledge that it is always in the moment of choosing that our outcomes are revealed.

{CHOICES}

They are often questioned: will I regret or resent what I have chosen, am I happy with the outcomes, will I sit comfortably with **the** way they have steered my life? They **are** nesting inside, breathing life into its decision, stepping lightly on the brain until it pounds its way out, echoing our findings to the world.

{CHOICES}

A decision, followed by an action, then revealed to all. Turning the pages of our countless thoughts, everyone questioned, disabling us of all reason.

CHAPTER SIX

WHY

{WHY}

It keeps us living in a constant state of complication, magnifying our hardship and discomfort.

{WHY}

It is time to stop asking and to rise above the question, to take responsibility and welcome whatever is concerning us without letting it tumble us into a tidal wave of emotion.

{WHY}

It is stubborn like a teenager, fighting us at every turn, taking ownership of the answers we crave, a battle between our reasoning and our desire. It denounces us, demanding we surrender to its power.

{WHY}

It is so difficult to pinpoint the answers we seek, that it is like reaching for a butterfly and grabbing nothing but air.

{WHY}

It strips us of the idea that we have any kind of control, as it manipulates all the thoughts we ponder, making us feel bare and vulnerable in the process.

{WHY}

We must step into the role of an observer of our life, safeguarding ourselves with hope. When following the question, we think we have received the explanation we so intently seek. It is often followed by yet another why, with no answer adequate enough to satisfy us.

{WHY}

It's the starting point to all of life's inquiries, the path we take toward understanding its meaning. We chase it like a marathon runner with no finishing line in sight, and no stamina strong enough to fight against its questioning power.

{WHY}

We send our questions off, expecting an immediate response, which seldom returns with our desired answer. Sometimes we wait for months and even years before we receive the answer we seek. We need to stop waiting and start living…

{WHY}

When we find ourselves in quicksand, with no branch in sight, we look to it to rescue us, to pull us out of our suffering. We worship it like an idol, craving some kind of understanding of our most complex concerns.

{WHY}

We hunt it with force, thinking that if it answers us, we will regain our control. We put pressure on it, wanting it to rescue us like a pound puppy waiting for a place to call home.

{WHY}

It is not our answers, it is not our questions, it is not our turmoil to clear our path—it is our faith that, no matter what the why, it will always lead us toward the explanation we seek...

{WHY}

The distance between our frustration and our answer is so wide that our questions often get blurred in the distance they travel.

{WHY}

It is our most disconcerting yet most used word. We ponder it, we question it, we argue with it, and we often challenge with doubt and suspicion the answers we receive.

{WHY}

We continue to chase it for the answers we need. We want peace and certainty, but it is masked in the delusion that it will set us free.

{WHY}

It robs us of our dreams and questions our choices. We seek to understand it, to give it a reason to reveal its explanation.

{WHY}

The answers are buried so far inside of us that even after years of digging, we cannot reach them.

{WHY}

We must stop giving it power and let it go! In the end, perhaps it is not our why that needs to be answered, but God's. We need to stop questioning our outcomes and turn over our concerns to Him, knowing with absolute confidence that it is His Why, not ours, that we need to lean in to.

{WHY}

The question follows all our hardships, leaving us chained to our difficulties and discontentment. It magnifies our problems, anchoring us to cement flooring—stuck—with no escaping its magnitude of disruptions.

{WHY}

Like a rapid burning fire, it sparks worry and doubt within us, pounding like a drum on our mind with no rhythm ample enough to carry us home.

{WHY}

It shapes us by the answers it offers, and molds us into the human beings we become by the countless understandings that it reveals.

{WHY}

It's an overwhelming force that triggers all of our suspicions, circulating negative thoughts in our mind. We ask it of our parents, our friends, and God. We believe the response to "Why is this happening to me?" will fix everything, when truly it has never had the power to do so.

{WHY}

It is the glue that sticks to our every question, the weight of all our worries.

{WHY}

It's our prelude to the many questions asked. It is also the most considered word when asking about our most heart-wrenching tragedies. It trails after us, dictating the outcomes of our experiences.

CHAPTER SEVEN

TIME

{TIME}

It drifts by like a balloon floating in midair with a beckoning string, teasing us to think we can reach it or figure it out like a riddle needing to be solved.

{TIME}

We measure the depth of our aging by the reflection that stares back at us, counting the lines on our face like the trunks of the trees that stand before us.

{TIME}

Moment by moment we give birth to the idea that somehow, we can freeze it, without considering its future melting.

{TIME}

This freely given gift is often overlooked, even hidden, until we allow it to rise to the surface at the exact moment it needs to be shared.

{TIME}

Only in its appreciation do we start to understand where we began and where we will end. Time is truly an offering not to be discounted, taken advantage of, or misused. It is to be cherished, celebrated and most importantly, lived to the utmost.

{TIME}

The magnitude of aging cannot be manipulated; it creeps in and slowly takes over. We search for our youth through products, considering the approval of others, resisting rather than embracing its coming.

{TIME}

In our youth, we were in a hurry to appear older, to age instantaneously. We took for granted the long summers that awaited us, not realizing what a momentary and fleeting gift we had.

{TIME}

We dig deeply into our thoughts trying to figure it out, make sense of it, face its mystery head on. We take for granted our special moments, not always cherishing them for the treasures they are. We cannot hide or escape from it. We wish to seize it, capturing its essence and discoveries that we find in the proceedings.

{TIME}

We view our bodies, not for the amazing gifts that they are, and for their durability in supporting us over the years. Instead, we focus on our disapproval, feeling like the seasons have not treated us kindly. Our physical condition gradually ages, and how easily we forget that it has offered us strength and beauty throughout our multitude of intervals.

{TIME}

It's always measured, and we often question it, as we forever ponder it in our mind: do we have enough, how should we spend it, or how do we make the most of it? It is the one constant challenge we can never completely conquer.

{TIME}

It is in our youth that we experience a keen desire to mature quickly, yearning to speed up the clock. Then suddenly, we reach a moment of maturity where we wish to slow it down, to back up the years, to embrace once again a slice of our callow self.

CHAPTER EIGHT
WORRY

{WORRY}

It's astute and silent and wiggles its way into our decision process. Impactful, demanding us to reflect on the damage it has elevated with the energy we have given to it, confidently knowing that its disruptions have rattled our life.

{WORRY}

It's out of reach, like a kite flying up to the sky with a ribbon trailing behind it—always there, teasing us with its influence, weaving its way into our existence.

{WORRY}

When anchored in our presence, it can feel like quicksand pulling us beneath the earth's surface with no twine to extricate ourselves from its domination. If we allow it to lead us, we will be left with nothing but it, like trees in the midst of winter—bare and empty.

{WORRY}

We need to lead with our hearts and let our minds go to a place of comfort and certainty. Let go of the trash that takes up space in our minds; watch it disappear like a feather that blows in the wind with no destination in mind and nowhere to land.

{WORRY}

We don't desire it, but it pursues us in the most unassuming way and, before we know it, we are allowing it to control us. It pretends to care, to show us that its mindset will protect us, but it is a false security—it is deadweight, not a line pulling us forward.

{WORRY}

It finds a way to enter at our weakest
point, ready to nag us with its beliefs—
like a storm that never stops, changing
our conditions, demanding that we look
further inside ourselves for shelter.

{WORRY}

It strips us of all logic, weakens our mind and manipulates all our concerns as it shoots down our certainty by the power it has over us.

{WORRY}

It is a thief stealing our time, acceptance and confidence. We know better and we know that if we cling to it, it will ultimately bring bad news in many configurations.

{WORRY}

It injects us with irritation followed by mental chatter bearing a mind-scrambling reality. We try to dodge it like balls on a court; we run, we hide, we pretend it does not exist. It disguises itself as caring but cleverly strips us of our certainty.

{WORRY}

Intriguing at first, we don't recognize it, as it is cunning in its approach, building momentum to swoop in and take charge of our every thought. It's perceived as concern, but that is just a glance into the uneasiness that accompanies it.

{WORRY}

If we choose to walk with it, over time it will paralyze us. Every moment it comes to visit, we need to practice guarding ourselves against it like an impenetrable cement wall. Then, over time, it will drift off into the distance like the clouds that move slow-and-steady toward the horizon, disappearing permanently from our thoughts.

{WORRY}

We must stop opening ourselves up to it, knowing the residual outcome. We often utilize it when wishing our loved ones to be safe or when questioning the choices we have made. Our mind wanders to it when we think about our health and safety. We should lean into faith and not give any power to uncertainty, removing its influence forever.

{WORRY}

It is like a rodent gnawing our insides with the anxiety it devises. It starts a tug-of-war of seduction, pushing its way into our mind, battling us for control. It hides behind concern and doubt, ready to drag us into unwanted drama.

{WORRY}

We need to release it, let it go, like a bird in flight heading in the opposite direction. Stay centered in peace, faith, hope and trust that everything will work out, confidently knowing we are always and forever protected by the light of the Lord.

{WORRY}

We know deep inside that the outcomes that follow are seldom positive. It stalls our progress with hesitation and cements us to the uncertainty we fear most.

{WORRY}

If we allow ourselves permission to live in faith, we will keep our joy and revive all the gifts the Lord intended us to utilize. Then we can begin to experience the life He intended us to live, which is far greater than our worries could ever manifest.

{WORRY}

It is like a thief; it jumps in, takes over and steals our time with its presence. It is elated by the control it assumes over our judgment.

{WORRY}

It can deplete our sleep, take away our appetite, or make our insides burn. Still, if we relinquish our power to it, we will lose that battle and it will take up space from our hopes and minds.

{WORRY}

It can make us sick, make us panic, or make our heart miss a beat. It can give us gray hair and wrinkles and age us by the thoughts it brings. It is wasteful, because when it influences our actions, we cannot be productive. We question our beliefs and lose trust in our intuition.

MANIPULATION

{MANIPULATION}

When centered in it, it makes us believe
our opinions are exceptional, like an
actor bowing on stage after a grandiose
performance yet lacking any real talent
that would warrant applause. It lacks
empathy and is absent of understanding.

{MANIPULATION}

It's fueled by misbehavior, turning our dialogue into emotional pain, steering us toward eliminating those who get in our way.

{MANIPULATION}

It arrives discreetly, like a cloud floating
by slowly, with whispers of what to say.

{MANIPULATION}

It delivers our words with the force of a tornado destroying everything in its path. Its motivation is to prove a point, and it's always functioning from ego with no regard for anyone's feelings but its own.

{MANIPULATION}

It's disingenuous in its approach, revealing only that which it wishes to disclose. It favors the ego and seeks the "me monster." Its prized triumph is determining that for which we ache, then pinpointing our motives to align with it.

{MANIPULATION}

We reject the affliction that it has planted in us. We take responsibility for being oblivious to its true nature and for blaming others when we lost sight of our own reasoning.

{MANIPULATION}

It is persuasive in the way it sneaks into our character ever so gradually, sparking blame, and before we know it, it is part of our existence through our words and our merciless actions.

{MANIPULATION}

The disruption it has brought into our lives dominates us, with the upsetting influence and inner conflict we face by its negative nature.

{MANIPULATION}

It starts with small lies, which mature over time into deceptive behavior. It operates from flattery, making its way into our logical thinking. It's indirect in the beginning and if we allow it, it will forcefully transform the kindness within us.

{MANIPULATION}

When partnering with it, we exhibit an obsession for power and attention. It instills in us a demanding sense of entitlement, followed by lies, jealousy and even rage when the outcome is not what we crave.

{MANIPULATION}

The moment we enter this world with our fists clenched, it's introduced to us by the ingenious way it leverages its power. It begins by nudging us to cry as a means of communicating our desires for food, comfort and love. It is our first glance at seeing the power it possesses.

{MANIPULATION}

Its intentions are entrenched in corrupt behavior, a weapon that harms others, twisting our words, cutting to the core, and depleting all the kindness that was once there.

{MANIPULATION}

We have fought for our boundaries, safeguarding ourselves from its handling, and now there is no need for its domineering direction.

{MANIPULATION}

It attaches itself to our every word, sometimes revealing our conniving self to the public. Then, before we know it, if we allow it to influence our life, we are lying, cheating and betraying those we love by the actions to which it attaches itself.

{MANIPULATION}

It possesses our souls and darkens our hearts. We are all infected by it; neither humans nor animals can escape its primal influence. It's sneaky in its execution, and if we open ourselves up to it, cruelty will be at the forefront of our character.

{MANIPULATION}

It's time to break the spell it cast upon us many years ago, to grow deaf to its buzzing mental chatter and its evil suggestions.

{MANIPULATION}

It sneaks into our thoughts, clearly determining that for which we yearn, in order to rule the many pleasures we crave, dominating our every thought with destructive logic.

{MANIPULATION}

It provokes wickedness and fights with our kind nature, as our goodness is the only thing that can overcome its power and its ability to rule our communications.

{MANIPULATION}

It is understood that it is not always deceitful, and we recognize that if our desired outcome is seeded in doing good, it can be a useful tool, and for that, we should be thankful.

{MANIPULATION}

We need to recognize it when it comes to the surface. It's important to no longer hear its suggestions or accept those visions it proposes to our mental picture. We have the power to rise above it, to lead ourselves with grace and humility. It's time to call it for what it is and cut it out of our lives for good!

{MANIPULATION}

We do not see it revealing itself at first, as it slowly invades us with its presence, prompting our first tantrum as a child. It increases its significance into our adulthood, when it insists that we use its influence to gain power, to get a job, or to fall in love. Before we know it, if we are not careful, it is at the forefront of all our discussions.

{MANIPULATION}

When we allow its influence, our words take flight, as it harnesses the effect of our altercation by spreading its desired message driven by greed.

{MANIPULATION}

It takes ownership of our soul, infects
us, ransacks our goodness and knocks
us down until we are nothing but cruel.

{MANIPULATION}

It presents us with devious ways to wield people for our advantage. We do not fully understand the power of it in the beginning, but we do know that if we adopt it as our mentor, we will have more power to gain what it is that we most desire. But, be careful, if we are not cautious, it will rule us with its wicked ways.

{MANIPULATION}

We must guard ourselves against it! If we are not mindful, it can inject poison so deeply into our story that we are in danger of becoming narcissistic and revealing our inflated ego.

{MANIPULATION}

After many seasons, we have awakened to an understanding of the destructive behavior it has unleashed in us, changing the living soul we have grown into. We no longer wish to be the individual we see in our reflection, the one it helped shape.

{MANIPULATION}

It slides into our innocent state of mind.
We call upon it to get what we desire
from the very moment we learn to speak.

CHAPTER TEN
CHANGE

{CHANGE}

We must learn to welcome it, to embrace
it and to let it breathe where air is needed.

{CHANGE}

It's uncertain; it comes in the darkness of the night or the rise of the day, continuously challenging us to stall it like an engine not ready to drive forward.

{CHANGE}

It can remodel our life, addressing our fluctuating moods, extracting the cemented footing that keeps us stagnant.

{CHANGE}

It can be troublesome, removing us from all our comfort and familiarity. It is taxing on our intellect and questions our reasoning and the laborious doubt of our choices.

{CHANGE}

It can be quick and unexpected or gradual and predictable. It cannot be bypassed or ignored, as it is forever pursuing us.

{CHANGE}

We look at our reflection and notice that the years have taken us hostage and our youth has been erased. We glance, and, in a flash, we notice the new markings of our physical being.

{CHANGE}

It is what pilots us to our next stage in life, pulling on our dreams and questioning our decisions. Life is a constant revision of the person we were and the person we are steadily becoming.

{CHANGE}

It arrives with introspection, challenging us to accept it or live in our current reality. We must embrace it and allow our story to be revealed.

{CHANGE}

Sometimes change is needed, sometimes forced and sometimes welcomed, but from wherever it is rooted, it results in the countless turnovers of our life.

{CHANGE}

It's clever and it camouflages itself in our moments, sneaking in when we least expect it. We need to embrace our crossings, gripping tightly to them without the fear of what is about to come next.

{CHANGE}

It shakes our life like a branch with loose leaves. It can turn our worry into unwanted anxiety and beat us, leaving us damaged and bruised from our resistance.

{CHANGE}

The transformation used to enter slowly, giving us abundant opportunities to catch up, to fit it into our current essence. We must welcome its effects and allow it to enter where it chooses.

{CHANGE}

It comes before we are ready and chases us like a queen bee buzzing around us while we anticipate its sting.

{CHANGE}

It dominates us, takes over and demands us to follow its lead in the direction it chooses.

{CHANGE}

We need to take a stance and move forward in it, honor it, accept it and, when it comes calling, invite it in and be delighted in its process, continuously delivering a tomorrow to our story.

{CHANGE}

It's living in a constant correction,
delivering new perspectives, emerging
from the many lessons learned.

{CHANGE}

We hope to govern it in the world, in our circumstances, and in the outcomes that await us. Still, it is the changes we make in our mind that ultimately are the most valuable.

{CHANGE}

It can ignite anticipation or enthusiasm, but either way, it will spark something in us to move forward.

{CHANGE}

It can be for our misfortune or our prosperity, but ultimately it will be. We cannot run from it, hide, or escape it, and if we fight it, it will be sure to bring hardship.

{CHANGE}

We stare at our family members who have aged before us, measuring our years by their appearance. We are constantly evolving and gaining new awareness by the truths presented in our current reflections.

{CHANGE}

Time has sped up, taken over and replaced our ability to gradually absorb it. We need to desperately search for a way to slow it down and secure our treasured moments.

{CHANGE}

We notice the change in our children as they grow quickly before us, shifting our perception and directing us to what's coming next.

{CHANGE}

We sense the change of seasons as the climate transitions. The sun rises, the snow melts, the rain falls, and the leaves change over in a multitude of colors. The weather, hot or cold, leads us to the transformation that will soon take place.

{CHANGE}

Whether the change is good or bad, it's constant and it will forever stand.

MOTHER EARTH

{MOTHER EARTH}

She is art; she is beauty; she is life's mystery revealed. As Mother, she is the center of everywhere and the compass of nowhere, encircling us wherever we go.

{MOTHER EARTH}

She hovers above all others, surrounds us, awakens us, and nurtures our soul. She declares her love in the beauty she lavishes on us. Her natural curves, colors, rhythm, and water, continually being renewed, reborn, and blossoming with each season she births.

{MOTHER EARTH}

Time spent with her is never wasted; it is impregnated with new perspectives. Every walk we take in her company is filled with the magnitude of her abundance, capturing the masterpiece lying above and below our living space.

{MOTHER EARTH}

She reveals her emotions woven into the seasons she presents to us. She invites us to explore her, to receive her, but most importantly to celebrate her vast contributions to our world.

{MOTHER EARTH}

Her form is alive, breathing, and existing through her powers of conception. Yet she depends on us to care for her creations and for their ultimate survival, so that she may live on, continuously blooming for our enjoyment.

{MOTHER EARTH}

Her stars awaken the sky, her rain falls as needed, her snow glitters before it melts, and her birds wave to us from high in flight. She is certainly enticing and blankets us in her creativity. She is diverse in temperature, often chilled, sometimes blazing, but forever changing.

{MOTHER EARTH}

She is caring, never hurried, never pushed to make plans. She plants seeds, delivers landscapes and patiently births life to all that surrounds us.

{MOTHER EARTH}

She softly harmonizes through the breeze and howls through the thunder; she weeps through the rain and rages through the oceans with immeasurable force. Her distant horizon engages us in the promise of a boundless beauty stretching endlessly before us.

{MOTHER EARTH}

She thrives in vitality at her roots, not allowing man to extinguish her, as she conceives under compulsion. She emerges anew each spring, her beauty coming alive with the brightness of her shining sun, illuminating the world.

{MOTHER EARTH}

Her magnificent creations sparkle in a multitude of colors, bountiful with life and a worldly pulse throbbing her unparalleled power.

{MOTHER EARTH}

She grows in silence, patiently renewing and uncovering her beauty. She embraces all living things, and the creatures she loves come to her for protection, food, and survival, and when her seasons transition, we know the next interval will closely follow.

{MOTHER EARTH}

She speaks to us in a very personal way; she is intimate in her connection, and grabs hold of our attention with every moment we experience in her presence.

{MOTHER EARTH}

She fights for us, keeping herself alive even when trapped by storms, earthquakes, or violent tornadoes; she is forced into combat, showing her fortitude to remain.

{MOTHER EARTH}

The living landscape she designs has been painted in brilliant colors, awakening the spirit of the earth. She yearns to be appreciated and loved, for humans to embrace her with their care and kindness.

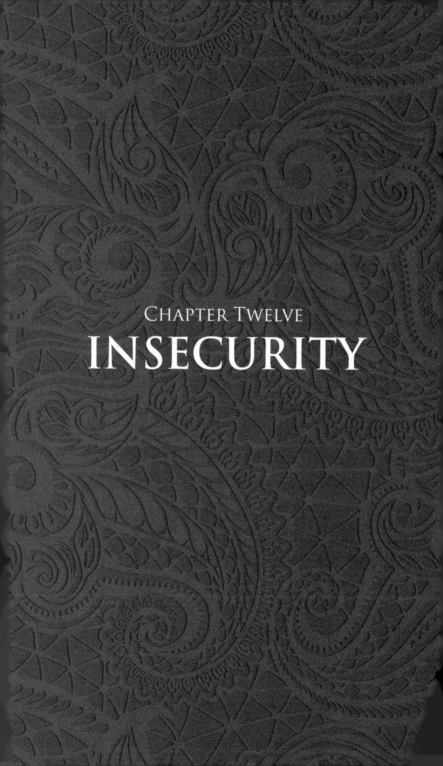

CHAPTER TWELVE

INSECURITY

{INSECURITY}

We take it personally, its deceptive messages that reflect back to us as discontent, absorbing its beliefs that it knows the truth about us. It's wicked in its delivery, casting a spell upon us to take its opinions to heart.

{INSECURITY}

It makes us feel exposed with the jealousy it triggers in us. It all begins and ends in the thoughts and false stories it implants into our minds, which continually play over and over making our mental picture permanent.

{INSECURITY}

It is like a long-term illness that kills us over time, hindering our spirit, infecting our joy and robbing us of our loving and self-accepting heart.

CHAPTER TWELVE

{INSECURITY}

It dims our light when we look in the mirror, until the moment it makes us want to cover ourselves and disappear.

{INSECURITY}

It points its finger at all our imperfections, draining us of our beauty. It's focused on the negative, always bringing to the surface that which we fear most, twisting our stomach in knots, binding us to its judgments.

{INSECURITY}

Let's take our power back! It is vital that we accept ourselves, love ourselves, then pause and reassess toward celebrating who we are.

{INSECURITY}

We must always remember to put forth our best intention toward self-care, loving our reflection and accepting thanks for our alluring qualities, highlighting the beautiful and amazing person that we are. If we focus on the positive and compliment ourselves often, we will find that we will readily welcome back our confidence.

{INSECURITY}

Day by day it tags us... "You're it," it proclaims, and it begins its chase: to disarm us, enforce its influence and change the way we identify ourselves, adding to the self-criticism we put upon our physical bodies.

{INSECURITY}

It is constantly molding us, changing our figure, conforming our structure toward the look it needs us to see. It longs to take every bit of attention away from us, preparing us for a disappearing act.

{INSECURITY}

It floods our tears and fakes our smile, threatening our joyful spirit. It is like a seed that does not need soil to grow, as it creeps around our heart like tangled vines strangling our confidence.

{INSECURITY}

It forces us to question our mind when doubt rules us and we are centered in uncertainty. When we conform to its way of thinking, we tend to question our worth and, as a result, it steals our happiness.

{INSECURITY}

It anchors us in fear, closing us off to our relationships with the threat of feeling pain, hurt, or loss, setting off a chain of crises that ultimately results in projecting and materializing that of which we are most afraid.

{INSECURITY}

It obscures us with doubt like darkness covers our light, so no one will see the sparkle within us, deepening our feelings of rejection.

{INSECURITY}

It hooks us, drawing our attention toward it and the power it has on our disappearing disposition. It is taxing on our morale and critical like an irate boss hollering in dissatisfaction.

{INSECURITY}

It is rambunctious at the root of its lies
and, before long, we start to believe them.
It butchers everything that is beautiful
within, activating us with doubt and fear
that we are not good enough.

{INSECURITY}

It pulls on us as if we are putty, stretching us in every direction, sparking our self-doubt, giving in to its power until we break.

{INSECURITY}

It is all-consuming at the forefront of our feelings. It takes ownership of our conflicting emotions, submerging them, until they spark confusion and negativity toward the false story that we tell ourselves.

{INSECURITY}

It takes our breath away, strangling us
by the negativity it seeds in our minds.

{INSECURITY}

When partnered with jealousy, it brings to the surface feelings of confusion accompanied by sadness, loneliness, uselessness and the heart-wrenching emotion of being invisible.

{INSECURITY}

It stops us from trying new things, from being courageous, by the corruption it drills in our hearts. It prompts social anxiety, negative beliefs about ourselves, and perfectionism. It opens our ears to judgmental and critical people who add to its strength.

{INSECURITY}

It uses our scale to torment us and demands we live in a constant state of comparison.

{INSECURITY}

It always positions itself at the front of the line, projecting its thoughts onto us and the way we perceive ourselves.

{INSECURITY}

Jealousy partners in everything it executes, so we seldom see them separate from one another—they give each other life and then project their collective convictions onto us.

{INSECURITY}

It is forceful in making us believe we are inadequate or less than deserving of self-love, as its amplified words weigh us down by the control it has over us.

{INSECURITY}

It feeds off bad behavior, jealousy and discontent as jealousy is its closest connection, wanting it to be first in our every thought.

{INSECURITY}

It is deceitful in its welcoming as it portrays itself to be a caring friend, sharing with us constructive criticism; truthfully, it's evil and like tar it sticks to us, sealing all our disappointing views about ourselves.

{INSECURITY}

It imitates the mirrors at the carnival, distorting our reflection, presenting us with a view we have never seen before. Changing the way we see our size, our height, our skin and our thighs.

{INSECURITY}

It arrives at the most inconvenient times, when we need to feel our strongest, visiting us in its petty approach, echoing laughter when diverting all our confidence.

{INSECURITY}

We must replace self-criticism with self-love, to live in our moments of accomplishments and award ourselves the praise we deserve for just being who we are—beautiful and perfect in our own unique way, the way God intended us to be.

{INSECURITY}

It takes from us what is rightfully earned, dividing our relationships by its influence. It focuses on our imperfections in our lonely moments and breaks our hearts in the way we do not love or celebrate ourselves.

{INSECURITY}

If we are not careful, it could eat us alive with the overwhelming feelings it implants in our minds of being unlovable, flawed, fragile and worthless.

{INSECURITY}

It has the predominating power of eliminating our confidence like a warden dominates his inmates who shrink under his care.

{INSECURITY}

We need to practice self-approval, self-love and joy to embrace non-comparison acts toward developing trust in who we really are.

{INSECURITY}

It's debilitating to our existence; it jumps up and down on our heart as though we were a trampoline, damaging our self-reliance and weakening our fighting power.

PAIN

{PAIN}

It demands us to reflect, to look within, to let go, and to allow healing to enter our space.

{PAIN}

It gives us the illusion of incomparable loneliness, overcome by worry at the slightest sign that it may return. It makes us want to guard ourselves from it, hide, and disappear from its prison. Its hidden motives wrestle with our exposed emotions, holding us back from the healing that's needed.

{PAIN}

It visits all of us, in different forms, and at different times. It comes in many configurations and, when it does, it transforms our days with amplifying power. It is often accompanied by sorrow and grief.

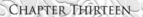

{PAIN}

When it digs deeper, gouging into our life, we must stifle the crushing mental noise that keeps us married to it. When we begin to understand that it is not self-inflicted, it loses its power.

{PAIN}

We can change our thoughts about it, choose a different response, and accept it, the growth, and development of more compassion, more empathy and even a brand-new courage in its process.

{PAIN}

We try to mask it, to erase the truth of
what we feel deep inside. We must learn
from the moments it has stolen from us.
When we are seated in it, we are broken
like shattered glass, caught in midair
with nowhere to land.

{PAIN}

It's fickle and unpredictable, and we never know when it will confront us with its presence. God, pleadingly trying to reach us in our pain; He continues tenderly with His unseen presence. There is hope, just believe that this is temporary.

{PAIN}

It will in time transfuse courage, strength and perseverance when we decide that the process implies that we are being prepared for something larger. It requires awareness, growth and, above all else, patience.

{PAIN}

We cannot let it triumph; we need to muster our strength and fight to gain precious ground. Even a small seed must be buried in the dirt before it breaks through to see the light of day. We must first learn to live in the darkness before we welcome and celebrate living in the light.

{PAIN}

It is cruel, critical and debilitating to our emotions. It robs us of our hope and challenges our certainty. It depletes our belief in ourselves and protests our self-acceptance.

{PAIN}

It does not matter in what embodiment it appears; it is destructive and leaves a path of despair and anger in its season of suffering.

{PAIN}

It crushes our world, leaving us feeling alone and saddened. It is exhausting, a true thief of our energy, leaving us beaten from its presence.

{PAIN}

It weighs heavily on our heart, heavier with the multitude of seasons it spends with us. It disguises itself, ready to dive into our life at any given moment, causing us to stumble and fall. It tests us, challenges us to be ready for it, not to be reactionary, but to build more strength for the next time it visits.

{PAIN}

Sometimes it is so excruciating, so violent to our souls, that we feel crippled inside, afraid to take a step toward healing.

{PAIN}

The tragedy of our agony is our vulnerability as we seek to be understood, comforted and supported. When we sit with it, we feel completely abandoned, as though we are the only ones in the world left in its company.

{PAIN}

It's time to ignore it, to let it go, to celebrate its exit. Let's welcome a new excitement and satisfaction, knowing that healing will take its place. It can be replaced with pure joy, blessings beyond reason, and a newfound courage in the glory of just being alive.

{PAIN}

We experience it through loss, hurt, and horrendous heartache, both emotional and physical. It turns our world upside down, shaking us to the core, kidnapping our joy, and raping us of all hope.

MUSIC

{MUSIC}

It communicates to our soul what our ears are too shy to receive. The notes enhance our appreciation, orchestrated in perfect harmony. It gives life to all that is shared, expressed and understood; packed with pleasure, embraced in lyrics, overcome by spirit.

{MUSIC}

It can spark reflection, inflict pain and touch the wounds of our past. When words fail us, the music can sing what our heart and mind feel beneath the surface.

{MUSIC}

It descends upon a broken heart, a breakup, or an emotional examination. It can also spark the memory of something sentimental—a first dance, a first kiss, or a celebration. It's our beginnings and endings woven into a lifetime of tunefully scripted moments.

{MUSIC}

The songs are what we feel deep inside,
holding them close and letting them go.
Lyrics are like flying notes that soar into
our ready ears to deliver the message,
and the stories that must be told, with
the many feelings that we must embrace.

{MUSIC}

It's our most irresistible kinship. A collection of feelings, emotional communication woven into verses, tunefully changing us forever.

{MUSIC}

It is the best account of history, a true measure of decades. It bleeds from our sorrows and dries our tears; it hugs our heart, keeping us together, or amplifies the sadness of being apart, always requiring us to share wherever the melody takes us.

{MUSIC}

It provides counsel and comforts us; it's imperative like the air we breathe, and critical to our understandings of our past and present. When words escape us, music picks us up, bringing our enjoyment home.

{MUSIC}

The quieter we become, the more we can hear the notes embracing us, reflecting our thoughts, connecting with the tunes that play for our enjoyment...And when it's impossible to be silent, we sing.

{MUSIC}

It grants a heart to the universe, meaning to the mind, flight to the artistry, air to its imagery, and life to all things. When we connect to it, it can grip us, and the song can take ownership of our soul.

{MUSIC}

It is the key to the house of all our understandings, transferring our complicated emotions and exposing them to the surface. When we fail to collect our feelings, music speaks the answers we need to hear.

{MUSIC}

It's a platform where words wander in like a stream of water flowing freely to its listener.

{MUSIC}

It gives us a glimpse into knowing the value of hearing it. It's an expansion constantly persuading us to tune in more intently.

{MUSIC}

It will always live on and be a vital part of our lives, with the notes in our hearts, the words imprinted in our minds and the songs instilled in our consciousness.

{MUSIC}

We meet our experiences in the lyrics we hear, creating a relatable common ground and gaining a better understanding of our own personal stories.

{MUSIC}

It can spark sadness or happiness, demanding we take notice, quiet our mouth and open our mind. It's our way of respecting the artistry and listening to its mastery.

{MUSIC}

When we sit and listen, the stories of the writer feed our soul, causing us to feel pregnant and empty at the same time, always wanting a different reality than the one we are living. We need to open our heart, as those who listen receive the gift of really hearing it. The songs clear our consciousness and refresh our memories.

{MUSIC}

It can expose the feelings we hold deep inside us and expand the understanding we all seek. The notes played are the universal stories we all share, which are amplified in the songs we hear.

{MUSIC}

It safely explores our complicated feelings. We worship, we listen, we applaud, and we stand with rapt attention to acknowledge the artist that stands before us. It is exceptionally important to our world, as it brings people together, universally crossing cultures.

{MUSIC}

It will never stop playing as long as we continue to validate the importance it plays in our life, and keep offering our accepting and loving ear.

{MUSIC}

It is a vocalization that every human being can understand; no matter the country or the language, it can be significant. Where communication fails, and our words get tangled in our feelings, music can pull us out of our darkness, supplying us with the answers we seek.

{MUSIC}

We can sit alone with it, share it, drive or dance to it, weep and giggle with it. It can trigger a moment in our history, it can rewind joy, pause happiness, and play peace; it can make us recall sadness or prompt laughter, but ultimately it will demand our soul to sing.

{MUSIC}

When we listen without judgment, letting ourselves feel the beat, our body can match the rhythm of our dancing spirit.

{MUSIC}

A world without it is silent, empty and detaches us from all connections. The beat pounds vibrations into a newly discovered way to express ourselves, keeping us alive in our empty moments.

CHAPTER FIFTEEN
SUFFERING

{SUFFERING}

We know deep down it is our greatest teacher, as it challenges us with the most heart-wrenching lessons. It drags us around until we are almost lifeless, centered in pain and crying its name. It is most powerful in our weakest state, when we are left with nothing but the choice to surrender to its will.

{SUFFERING}

It has placed us in a holding pattern, confusing our thoughts and our certainties, nagging us with highly offensive verbal jabs of distrust, questioning all we knew to be true before it infused our life with pain.

{SUFFERING}

It steals our hope and challenges our mental state, triggering a war of darkness, a combat that cannot be won. It shreds our body to its extremities, scorches it with scars, as we endure in silence.

{SUFFERING}

It anchors us by the weight of its strain and the severity of pain and uncertainty it infuses into our life. It has us questioning our every thought, finding ourselves shaken and directionless.

{SUFFERING}

Our minds swirl with worry, and our emotions are in a constant state of frustration as to why. If we hold on too tightly, or shove our resentments down too deep, we will become enraged, and our bodies will begin to scream in torment when anything else arises. This provokes us to run from our feelings instead of leaning into them, allowing them to naturally dissipate.

{SUFFERING}

It takes pure honesty to recognize it, to question our reality when it is taking up so much space. We receive warnings that it is about to surface, changing the outcomes that we will experience in our season of struggle.

{SUFFERING}

We try to hide our wounds from the world we live in, as if our bodies were in a bad collision and are beyond repair. Its damage has left us anxious and emotionally shaken, pushing and pulling on our foundation until there is no more vitality to abduct.

{SUFFERING}

It's like a vicious bear clawing at our insides with sharp paws, scratching its way out, tearing at our nucleus with every strike. The result and impact it has on our lives are dreadful. It's always instilling a feeling of being powerless and weak as it destroys us at the core of our being.

{SUFFERING}

It lives around the corner, ready to come out the moment someone we love dies or we get sick or injured. It's always close by if we have a heartbreak or a tragedy. We know now that we will all experience its presence in our lifetime, as there is no escaping it without being affected by the pain it has implanted into our season.

{SUFFERING}

It challenges our strength by the constant pain it plants in us. It ties our insides into knots and bleeds our ulcers by the fears it sparks in our hearts.

{SUFFERING}

It has accompanied our experiences with agony, and we have withstood the pain it has burst into our life. You see, it is a disguised gift, one that has made us fight for our joy, fight for our peace of mind, fight for our strength, and fight for our faith. It is now our time to rise above and for that we are grateful. It no longer has power here. We are turning our backs to it, abandoning it, as it is nothing but the ashes of our pain!

{SUFFERING}

It commands us to take on too much distress, much more than we are capable of carrying. The pain that trails us is like a damaged knee with scars so deep and damaging that no healing can begin.

{SUFFERING}

When we remove the disturbance it has stored in our mind, and the strain it has permeated in our body—only then can we begin to pursue hope, faith and forgiveness, which will liberate us, aborting the power it once held over us.

{SUFFERING}

It diminishes all that we believe by blinding us to any faith that may exist within us, robbing us of the comfort that was meant for us. It requires us to be in a constant state of defense, to be reactionary with no fighting power and no will to move forward.

{SUFFERING}

It confines us to our circumstances with no light in sight to show us when the nightmare might end. We are saddened by the way it demands us to question our faith and harden our hearts each time it visits.

{SUFFERING}

When it surfaces, we are stuck in a deep, dark hole, feeling frightened and alone. It ignites our insides, like boiling water, scarring and burning us.

{SUFFERING}

We are beaten down, feeling bruised by its time spent with us. It binds us to emotional turmoil and devours us in our season of sorrow.

{SUFFERING}

We know that it cannot resist grace forever; we must take the opportunity to grow beyond it, to plant another seed and start a new beginning. The time has come to stand firm, to emerge and become stronger and more advanced human beings.

{SUFFERING}

We do not have to live in its world or be stuck in its presence. We will fight, pull ourselves up, and stand with courage when our mind debates between despair and happiness.

{SUFFERING}

It's the handgrip wrapped around our neck, strangling us, until there is no longer air to breathe. It has been our experience that when it enters our life, it always outstays its welcome and leaves a trail of destruction and misery!

{SUFFERING}

It is evil at best. It restrains our spirit by the darkness that exists in it, and it drags us through the mud for its pleasure. It tortures us and turns our world upside down. It popularizes tears and triggers depression from the agony it implants into our circumstance, leaving us tumbled and torn, losing our footing on shaky ground.

CHAPTER SIXTEEN

PICTURE THIS

{PICTURE THIS}

We have a false attachment to our camera—we surrender ourselves to it, giving into the temptations for using it. The device triggers doubt and insecurities, demanding us to question our beauty, our size and our smile. We blame our conditions, the angle, the light, the height of the picture. It's a disappearing act from who we really are.

{PICTURE THIS}

We should never grant ourselves permission to live a false life. We need to open our eyes and close the lens to observe who we are, not worse, not better, but the certainty that we parade.

{PICTURE THIS}

The camera is a thief to our time, taking our pictures, viewing, editing and posting them. Hours and the days spent on social media looking for likes, for validation, giving away ourselves to others in the hopes of rising our own self-importance.

{PICTURE THIS}

When we lose touch with our authentic self, letting the image define us, we confuse the meaning of what it reveals about us. When we try to control the picture, it changes the outcome and our moments will be tarnished forever.

{PICTURE THIS}

When the camera looks at us through its lens, we can't truly be seen, as it cannot capture the essence of our natural beauty. The moment we click, we know the image can be changeable, we give in to our false sense of self, catering to the departure of our integrity.

{PICTURE THIS}

The camera is like a mirror measuring our maturity, our declining beauty, boomeranging our new reality in the picture we see, enveloped often in disappointment as to what we notice looking back at us.

{PICTURE THIS}

It's time to clear our perceptions of whom we think we have to portray, and when we give up the perfection we are seeking, we can then begin to expand being truly alluring and original.

{PICTURE THIS}

Stop waiting for the perfect image, as nothing in this life is perfect. It's all the imperfections woven together that make up true, authentic beauty.

{PICTURE THIS}

The camera device is becoming an addiction, and we are anxious to set it down for the fear that we will miss the moment to snap, instead of actually living happily in our moment.

{PICTURE THIS}

The picture makes us question ourselves: should we show our truest side, our innate beauty, or allow the misconception of our truest self to be presented, exposing only that which we think the world wants to see?

{PICTURE THIS}

It is time to give up the need to deliver more than is expected of us and give way to what is real. After all, to truly appear beautiful, we have to accept our flaws, our imperfections, and welcome our beauty without the need to measure it by the consent of others. Stop waiting for the perfect selfie and start living the perfect life.

{PICTURE THIS}

We show the camera what we want it to see. We smile for it, we pose for it, we put on makeup for it. We lure the camera, moving our bodies toward it, looking deep into its lens as though we are staring into the eyes of our lover.

{PICTURE THIS}

The camera is impregnated with all our memories, taking ownership of them, holding them captive, for us to rely on. It's fickle and faithful at the same exact time but can easily lose interest, pointing another way.

{PICTURE THIS}

The camera chooses its form, measuring history and continuously telling a story. It captures life, sunsets, landscapes, and celebrations, documenting time and our most treasured memories, which it holds safely for our future enjoyment.

{PICTURE THIS}

When we give way to both good and bad, nothing is hidden, and the more truths shared, the more we start to genuinely care. We need to stop comparing, competing and criticizing, because in the end, if we are focused on the approval of others, we will become caged by their opinions.

{PICTURE THIS}

We are taught at a young age to smile for the camera, to look at it playfully, to engage in its pull. It commands attention, fakes our smile and can invade our soul.

{PICTURE THIS}

We keep our picture devices with us at all times; we worship them, we feel connected to them, and we feel lost without them. It's the gateway to being overexposed; when we only see things and people of beauty, other things begin to appear ugly in their natural state.

SELF-LOVE

{SELF-LOVE}

It is a natural discovery that takes place over time. It invites us to become more of who we truly are, to magnetically pull ourselves closer to the mysteries that we must uncover and see clearly— the things others may never have the privilege to see if we don't.

{SELF-LOVE}

The enlightenment of our spirit demands
both our gratitude and our willingness
to receive the gifts our spirit brings us.
We must respect, nurture and embody
our best self as we are deserving of that!

{SELF-LOVE}

We must love ourselves first, so that we know what we truly desire and ultimately deserve. We must lead with our heart, as no amount of love from another is ever sufficient enough to fill the longing in our own soul.

{SELF-LOVE}

It is in our exploration that we find the source of who we were born to be and what role we play for others to see.

{SELF-LOVE}

Remember that insecurities and ego spark our doubt and fuel our attention toward negative self-talk. Share an enlightened conversation with yourself, filled with positivity, and then dive deeply into the acceptance, beauty and gifts that you possess.

{SELF-LOVE}

It's time to silence that inner critic; forgive ourselves, protect ourselves, and first, always and forever love ourselves, because if we don't, no one will ever see us close enough to value the gift in being who we truly are.

{SELF-LOVE}

Acceptance cannot accompany judgment or rejection, as they cannot coexist. Women have to stop hiding their most valuable and bare self or dim their light in order to gain approval.

{SELF-LOVE}

It allows us to give to ourselves our own loving attention. We are worth quiet time and reflection without any feelings of guilt. Let's start by talking to ourselves as we would to someone we love—with respect and admiration.

{SELF-LOVE}

In viewing our reflection, we should not sell ourselves a false or incomplete image. We should all allow a peek within, a precious moment of exploration, see an authentic picture of our self, framed in nothing but love.

{SELF-LOVE}

It is the compass to the needs of the heart, guiding us toward the natural progression of acceptance.

{SELF-LOVE}

When we are asked what do we care about, why is it that our own needs of the heart come last? If we do not love, respect and treasure every inch of our own being, then how can we expect another to notice or celebrate the uniqueness we bring to the world?

{SELF-LOVE}

Why dim our light when it was destined to shine? Acceptance is the truest form of beauty; it's how we feel about ourselves, not what we see in our reflection. We should reveal our most authentic self and watch the rest of the world open their eyes to see us, too.

{SELF-LOVE}

Be the person who is comfortable, confident and accepting of themselves, the one who holds themselves to their highest manifestation, the one who stands so firmly, so solidly, that outside opinions do not deter their happiness.

{SELF-LOVE}

Introduce the concept by embracing all that is uniquely special within, celebrating every inch, as it is worth our admiration. After all, the way we carry ourselves is the way the world sees us.

FAITH

{FAITH}

It's the step we take into a higher realization. Those who worship will hear the explanations they seek, which reflect the light and voice of the Lord in a clearly defined sign, erasing all past doubts.

{FAITH}

We cannot see it, as it is invisible like the air we breathe. We question it when we are struggling but when embraced, it brings forth a calming presence.

{FAITH}

We cannot demand the Lord's response, as it is His timing that we must embrace. We need to recognize all the times He has answered and be patient, knowing that the "why" may become clear only after we release it to God.

{FAITH}

It requires a closeness to God, and it is never rooted in hesitation or doubt, as it is the purest form of trust.

{FAITH}

It's vital to our existence, as important as the beat of our heart is to our living form; the union of soul is when we walk in wisdom, keenly aware of that which weaves our hopes with the Lord's unfailing love, dissipating any loneliness that we may have experienced as His love nurtures our spirit like the sun's rays nurture all.

{FAITH}

We need it the most when we are living in a state of frustration. It stretches us to go farther than we ever thought we were capable; we accept its influence beneath all our disbeliefs, like the pulse of the heart—silent but constant.

{FAITH}

In our seasons of adversity, when our thoughts are consumed by doubt, we must lean into faith despite our fears or confusion. The moment we accept that there is something greater than ourselves, we will begin to hear the universal whispers confirming that our prayers have been heard.

{FAITH}

We must inhabit it completely—jump in, like we would into a warm, welcoming pool—to liberate our soul. Each moment is fleeting and none of us are assured subsequent time; we must step toward the value that it holds, so we can radiate the exuberance of living with continuous contentment.

{FAITH}

It's living a life of grace where our kindness is welcomed, like a dog welcomes an embrace, and our words of hope reach the ears of those who are in need of the Lord's care.

{FAITH}

Faith is committing ourselves to prayer, inviting the Lord in with praise—open and wide-awake; calming our thoughts to hear the voice of reason even in our heartbreak; clearing our apprehension to trust Him; acknowledging the gift of His presence and the light that emanates from Him, igniting our own illuminated countenance to the world.

{FAITH}

From it we gain a subtle confidence that even when the world is in its darkest state we need not dwell on that which worries us, by prayerfully asking that our mind not reside in negativity. The obscurity we are feeling will be overpowered by the light of the Lord; we delight in the fact that love will conquer hate and rejoice in the cherished gift of life.

{FAITH}

Faith is insight to rest in the Lord's supremacy, to free ourselves from the human tendency to waste our energy on intolerable matters that we cannot control. It convinces us that light will triumph, harmonizing our hearts with any discordant or false apprehensions.

{FAITH}

Remember that when uneasy and barbaric thoughts entangle us, the reassuring words in the Lord's book make our earthly life less ominous; we know we are not alone and that His promises forever stand.

Chapter Nineteen
LETTING GO

{LETTING GO}

It's a human condition everyone struggles with, blurred by the emotional suffering to which we chain ourselves. Humanity is triggered by the knotted stresses we bear inside, followed by the troublesome moments we experience. It's time to release all our burdens like dispersing colorful confetti, which float up and land where needed.

{LETTING GO}

The moment we choose to release that which entangles us, we begin to open ourselves up to a new understanding and awareness, setting ourselves free, like a previously caged animal ready to run and live in a state of bravery.

{LETTING GO}

Before we mentally agree to it, a false narrative is played out in our mind; we question our motives and doubt that which is right for us. When we refuse, our feet are bound and our opportunities for growth are delayed.

{LETTING GO}

It's a choice that dictates the outcomes
of our story and triggers us to examine
our motives and discomfort, while
questioning our reasons; and when we
refuse, we carry it like a heavy burden,
weighing us down by its influence and
our defiance to move past it.

{LETTING GO}

We tell ourselves that we are okay, that we are not secretly inhibiting ourselves with past regrets, hurts and disappointments we combat internally. It's the imaginary war that resides in our distorted thinking. We must seek another perception, allowing our worries to travel to another place, to choose another destination, leading us out of obscurity and into the light of day.

{LETTING GO}

It's crucial to our survival, the starting point of our healing and the veracity of the fear lodged in our uncertainty. It's scary; it's giving up control, revealing our hidden scars and leaning into faith.

{LETTING GO}

When we refuse, we exist in a narrow tunnel of suspension, chained to our discomfort and ego, and the choice to not release will ultimately hinder our future outcomes.

{LETTING GO}

Release all the dwelling we have put on our past. Dismiss all the constant complaining, comparison, expectations and verbal self-sabotage. We do not need to hold on; we need to loosen our grip, give up our need for control, because if we don't hold on to that which bothers us, it cannot hold on to us.

{LETTING GO}

It frees us from what we have kept alive in our minds, which we have repeatedly played like the trailers of a movie for far too long. It commands us to forgive, to wipe clean the story we have narrated in our imagination, that battle which ceases our ability to move ahead.

{LETTING GO}

It's the shift in our awakening that begins our crossing. The starting point toward our processing, in which we train our mind to move forward, giving up the need to be attached to our past. When we resist, our grip is challenged and strained, like shackles on our ankles, enslaving us to our history and its pain.

{LETTING GO}

When we come to terms with it, it's like watching a dove in flight soaring toward peace with nothing but a clear path to joy. Our problems imprison us, as our mind is clever and captivating with its gripping demands.

{LETTING GO}

It's a compass toward the acceptance of who we really are. It's essential to heal our wounds; we have to stop our heart's bleeding from emotional turmoil and be resilient and cease the negative chatter we feed ourselves. We need to cut the rope that has kept us docked for far too long.

{LETTING GO}

Our mind spins in a constant state of dissatisfaction as we attempt to choke our resentments with a grip so tight that we become enraged, crying out in anguish and desiring to escape. Instead we need to lean in, observe and allow them to dissipate naturally.

CHAPTER TWENTY

REJECTION

{REJECTION}

It's the thing we most fear; our self-worth is tangled in it, yearning to belong, like our existence matters. It's facing our vulnerability and that which occupies our state of mind, spinning our thoughts and made-up truths, convincing ourselves to hold on tightly, to coddle ourselves against our wounds and our internal torment, damaging only ourselves in its process.

{REJECTION}

It triggers our deepest pain, damaging our self-worth and stinging us in places that the venom infinitely remains.

{REJECTION}

It endangers our confidence with the destructive criticism we interpret; we become entangled with our emotional and intellectual selves, fixated on the crushing influence it brings, hearing nothing but the dissatisfaction it has embedded in us. We must not allow someone else's opinion to dictate our value or allow our God-given light to be extinguished.

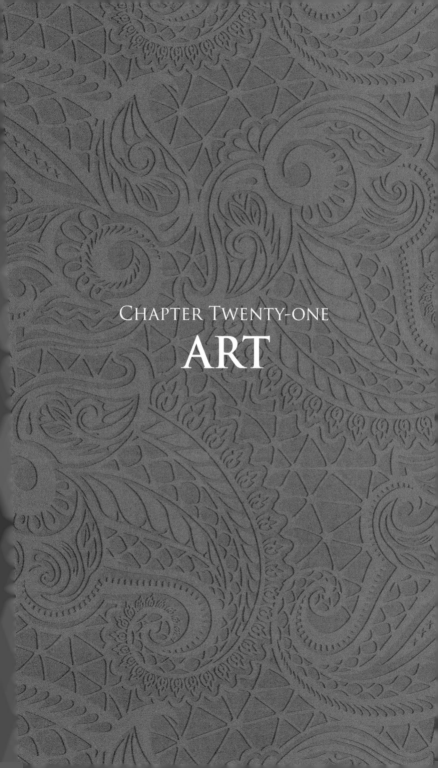

CHAPTER TWENTY-ONE

ART

{ART}

The moment we connect with art, our senses become heightened, by the monumental inspiration it presents. It can remove us from a stagnant life to a world where everything is possible.

{ART}

When artistry is conceived out of a personal interpretation, it challenges our assumptions because of the significance it has on us and our beliefs. We become consumed by the divine presence it evokes within us like a cerebral magnet.

{ART}

It's the experience that we all yearn for—something to make us feel, to relate to, to evoke feelings we did not know we had—which makes our world more accepting and beautiful.

{ART}

No other man-made object has such an effect on the mind and spirit. Art is a need, yes, a need to attach, a need to feel, a need to celebrate, and most importantly, a need to fall in love with something that speaks to our consciousness at its highest and deepest levels.

{ART}

It enhances our impression, our every emotion, allowing us to live it, to connect with it, and to celebrate its power.

{ART}

There are few things that consume our every sense, yielding us to stop and take notice, focusing all our attention toward the meaning behind the creation.

{ART}

Its magnetic pull draws observers to share their own intimate experience. It widens our cultural understandings and constantly inspires our confidence with the beauty surrounding us, torching a lasting impression.

{ART}

It influences our understanding, alluring us into a captivating story that is inspired to impact visual narrative.

{ART}

It opens our eyes to what each collector finds to be entrancing, kindling our own reflection and heightening an appreciation that has been there all along.

{ART}

The mentality it provokes, gives meaning to multiple worlds, connecting them at their core. It is always present within us, for once the creation is seen, it remains forever in our hearts and minds.

{ART}

As a gateway to new understanding, it nourishes us with stimulating elements, keeping our eyes from wandering because of the attention required to fully embrace it.

{ART}

It enables us to stand back from our own thoughts, by capturing our mind's eye, bringing into focus that which we need.

{ART}

It awakens a longing, knowing nothing is lost when a piece is found, with the understanding and depths it offers, effortlessly softening the stare. The true essence can rise up and meet us in our connection.

{ART}

It arouses within us a drive to understand
its thread of beauty, which echoes the
unparalleled desire it fuels inside us.

{ART}

We need it, without reason or justification; in return, it allows us to experience it freely, to speak honestly about what moves us, even when our brain resists.

{ART}

It takes us by surprise when we experience it, knowing that the magic will not slip away—the memory of it will be contained in multiple impressions that layer themselves in mental images we will forever commemorate.

{ART}

It is always true to the creator's vision; therefore, we do not have to change it, fix it, or mold it into a form that is different. It reveals its truest center in no particular way, without conveying any disappointment, judgment, or explanation to its beckoning.

ABOUT THE AUTHOR

DANIELLE TIANO is an author with a purpose: to help people overcome daily obstacles, enrich their lives and cultivate their growth. In her work, she draws from life's many complex emotions. Tiano's clarity of observation awakens a reader's understanding toward enlightenment, possibly forever changing the perceptions of her audience. An animated storyteller, her sincere love of the written word resonates through all of her work. Tiano had the honor of penning a customized book for the Los Angeles

Angels of Anaheim baseball franchise and Miller Children's & Women's Hospital titled *If You Want to Play...Eat the Right Way.* She also authored the *Temptation of a Generation* book series, which addressed the difficult task of opening discussions between parents and their children about cyberbullying, texting, and other internet-safety topics. Her work has been featured on the Dr. Laura Radio Show, Fox Sports West TV, KSL Studio 5 TV, and KDOC-TV. Her books have also been publicized on the Peter Anthony Holder Radio Show in Montreal, Canada, and Metroparent. com. In addition, Tiano was highlighted in the *OC Register*, *The Daily Pilot*, and *OC Family* magazine. She has been interviewed on radio and television as an influencer with impact, echoing her words to the masses. Danielle lives in Southern California with her husband and dog. She spends her time writing, bike riding, swimming, traveling the world, and doing charity work, which is dear to her heart.